Space Adventures

To Mars!

Gina Bellisario

illustrated by Mike Moran

M MILLBROOK PRESS • MINNEAPOLIS

For Sofia. I love you to
Mars and back! —G.B.

Millbrook Press
A division of Lerner Publishing Group, Inc.
241 First Avenue North
Minneapolis, MN 55401 USA

For reading levels and more information, look up this title at
www.lernerbooks.com.

Main body text set in Slappy Inline 22/28.
Typeface provided by T26.

Library of Congress Cataloging-in-Publication Data

Names: Bellisario, Gina, author. | Moran, Michael, 1957– illustrator.
Title: To Mars! / Gina Bellisario ; illustrated by Mike Moran.
Description: Minneapolis : Millbrook Press, [2017] | Series:
   Cloverleaf Space adventures | Audience: Ages 5–8. | Audience:
   K to grade 3. | Includes bibliographical references and index.
Identifiers: LCCN 2016010718 (print) | LCCN 2016012170
   (ebook) | ISBN 9781512425390 (lb : alk. paper) | ISBN
   9781512428322 (eb pdf)
Subjects: LCSH: Mars (Planet)—Exploration—Juvenile literature. |
   Space flight to Mars—Juvenile literature.
Classification: LCC TL799.M3 B45 2017 (print) | LCC TL799.M3
   (ebook) | DDC 523.43—dc23

LC record available at https://lccn.loc.gov/2016010718

Manufactured in the United States of America
1-41307-23251-3/4/2016

TABLE OF CONTENTS

Chapter One

A Red Dot

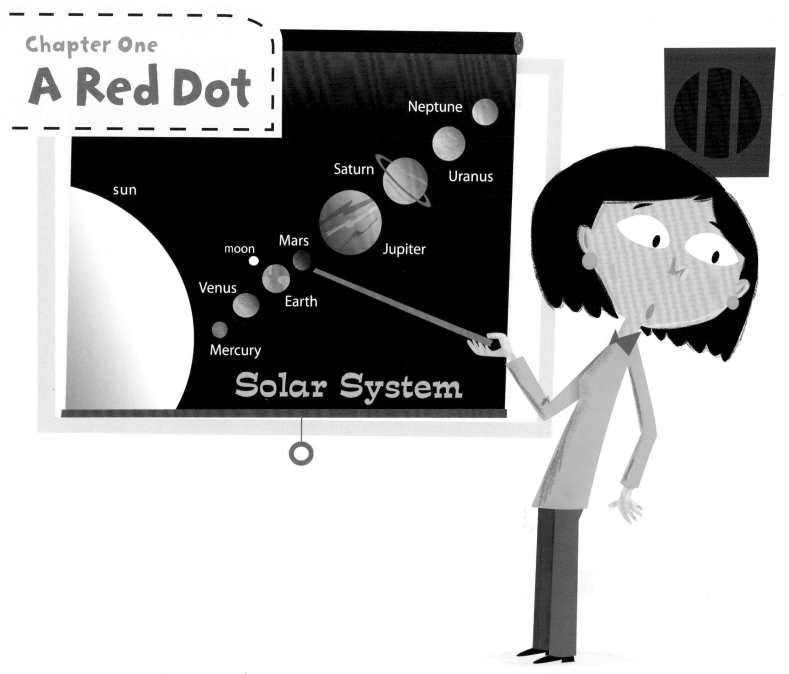

Ms. Cho said we were going to learn something fun today. Was she ever right! She points to a map of the solar system.

"Look! It's Mars!" I shout. "It's that red dot between Earth and Jupiter. It's my favorite planet!"

Everyone looks at me instead of Mars.
My cheeks turn as red as the planet.

"Wow, Avery! You're really excited to explore Mars," Ms. Cho says. "Out of all the planets, it's the most like ours. It has deserts and volcanoes, just like Earth."

Where is the largest volcano in our solar system? It's on Mars! Olympus Mons is so big that Hawaii's largest volcano and the rest of the Hawaiian Islands could fit inside it.

Mars sounds awesome. I'd love to see it for myself! But there's no way I can really go there.

So I close my eyes and just imagine what it's like on Mars. Then, all of a sudden . . . three, two, one . . .

BLASTOFF!

Chapter Two

Robot Explorer

Touchdown! Astronaut Avery has landed on Mars. Good thing I wore a space suit! Earthlings can't breathe on Mars easily. But that won't stop me from exploring!

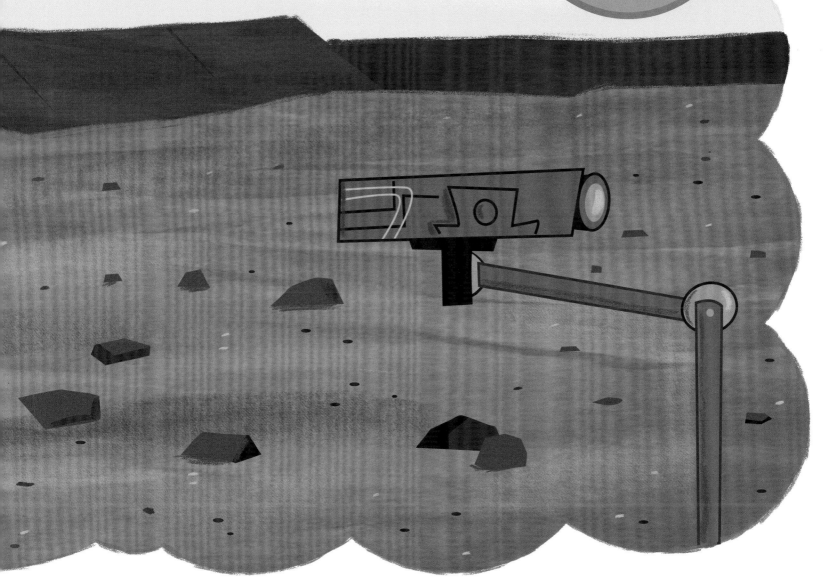

I guess I'm the only visitor from Earth. Or am I?

You don't need a space suit to breathe on Earth. The air is made of 21 percent oxygen. On Mars, it is less than 1 percent.

"Hi there!" says a friendly-looking robot. "I'm Rover. I'm on a mission to explore Mars. I collect information and send it back to scientists on Earth. This helps them learn about Mars."

NASA scientists send rovers to Mars. The rovers collect rock samples and take pictures.

It looks like I have an exploring partner.
High-five, Rover!

Chapter Three
Martian Basketball

Rover and I can't wait to go exploring. But just as we start out, a giant rock rolls into our path! "Warning: Rock ahead," says Rover.

Earth takes 365 days to orbit around the sun. Mars takes longer because it is farther away from the sun. A Martian year lasts nearly twice as long as an Earth year.

"I can try to jump over it," I say. I take a running leap and fly up, up, up!

"Mars is half the size of Earth," Rover reports. "That means its gravity is weaker. Here, you can jump three times higher."

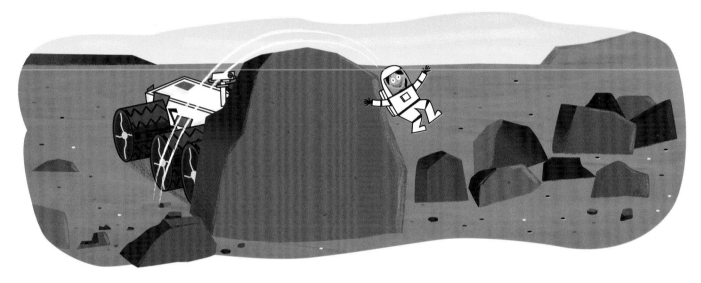

Maybe I can play Martian basketball!

Behind the rock, there are many more rocks just like it. They are part of a huge hill. That's where the big rock must have rolled from. "Let's go check it out, Rover!"

I climb up the hill, and Rover *r-r-r-umbles* up beside me. I want to show everyone that Rover and I once stood on this spot. I pull a flag out of my space suit and put it on the hill. It flaps around.

The wind on Mars can move as fast as a racing car. But it is thin and weak. It would feel like a breeze on Earth.

"Mars is windy," Rover says. "The wind creates huge dust storms."

Exploring Mars really blows me away!

Brrr! The air is cold. "I wish my space suit had earmuffs," I say.

"The average temperature on Mars is -80°Fahrenheit, or -62°Celsius," Rover explains. "Mars has four seasons like Earth. But summer feels like winter."

It's a good thing I left my swimsuit at home.
Still, is that water over there?

On a summer day, Mars can reach 70°F (21°C). But its atmosphere can't hold onto the sun's heat. When the sun goes down, the temperature can drop to -100°F (-73°C).

Chapter Four

Life on Mars?

"It IS water!" I shout.

"You're right!" Rover says. "Water exists on Mars. It may help us find life."

Scientists believe a special kind of salt water flows on Mars. While studying pictures of the planet, they noticed watery lines that went downhill. The lines appeared during warmer seasons and faded when the temperature cooled.

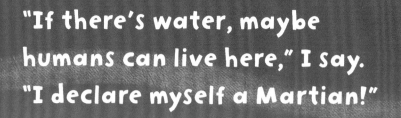

"If there's water, maybe humans can live here," I say. "I declare myself a Martian!"

Avery and Rover were here

1 the Martian

Then, all of a sudden, a voice says, "Astronaut Avery, return to Earth."

It's Ms. Cho! I open my eyes. I'm back in class.
"Time for recess, Avery!" Ms. Cho smiles. "Our lesson about Mars is done for today."

I'm sad to leave Mars, but it's good to be an Earthling too—especially today. It's my turn to pitch in kickball! And if I want to visit Mars again, it's only a daydream away.

Draw a Martian Home

Scientists think people will live on Mars by 2030. A home on Mars would look different from a home on Earth. Pretend you live in a Martian home. What does it look like? Draw it!

What You Will Need
two sheets of paper
a pencil
crayons or markers

How to Draw Your Martian Home

1) On one sheet of paper, make a list of what you need to survive on Mars. Include food, water, and a space suit. Mars is very cold, with large dust storms. Add something that will keep your home safe from the weather.

2) Use the other sheet to draw your Martian home. Food can't grow outside on Mars, so be sure to leave space for an indoor garden. And don't forget a place to park your spacecraft!

GLOSSARY

atmosphere: the gases that surround a planet

gravity: a force that pulls things toward one another

oxygen: a substance in the air that people need to breathe

rover: a machine that gathers information in space

solar system: a group of planets, comets, and moons that orbits the sun

BOOKS

JAN – 9 2018

Bloom, J. P. *Mars*. Minneapolis: Abdo, 2015. Learn about the air on Mars and the planet's size.

Furstinger, Nancy. *Robots in Space*. Minneapolis: Lerner Publications, 2015. Find out more about the robots that help scientists explore the solar system.

Markovics, Joyce L. *Mars: Red Rocks and Dust*. New York: Bearport, 2015. This book has photos of the planet's surface and tallest volcano. It also shares the differences between Mars and Earth.

WEBSITES

NASA: Mars Exploration
http://mars.nasa.gov/participate/funzone
This website is from the National Aeronautics and Space Administration. You can make your own paper spacecraft, explore a crater, and find out your weight on Mars!

***National Geographic Kids:* Mission to Mars**
http://kids.nationalgeographic.com/explore/space/mission-to
-mars/#mars-planet.jpg
Learn all kinds of facts about Mars. You can also look at a picture of its two moons, Deimos and Phobos.

PBS Kids—Design Squad: *Curiosity* Rover
http://pbskids.org/designsquad/video/curiosity-rover-mars
Landing the first rover on Mars was tricky. Watch a video and learn how engineers solved this problem.

LERNER e SOURCE™

Expand learning beyond the printed book. Download free, complementary educational resources for this book from our website, www.lerneresource.com.